The

I0176550

COURAGE

to

SERVE

**Inspirational Quotes for Servicemen
and Women**

Curt Thomas

www.CurtThomasSpeaks.com

The COURAGE to SERVE

ISBN: 978-0-9961977-2-4

Library of Congress Control Number: 2015904212

CURT THOMAS UNLIMITED, LLC Orangeburg, SC

www.CurtThomasSpeaks.com

The COURAGE to SERVE

The COURAGE to SERVE

www.CurtThomasSpeaks.com

Dedication

This book is dedicated to every man and woman who has serve or is currently serving in the Armed Forces: Active Duty and Reserves

Thank you for the sacrifices you've made for freedom of everyone. We don't say it enough but thank you...

The COURAGE to SERVE

www.CurtThomasSpeaks.com

USE

This quotes book is designed to be inspirational and motivational for the reader.

It is designed for you to read and re-read from time to time.

The hope of the author is for your consciousness to grow to reveal a different interpretation each time you read a quote in this book. Whether it's every day or once a week, motivation and inspiration is continual.

The COURAGE to SERVE

www.CurtThomasSpeaks.com

Quotes

The COURAGE to SERVE

"People sleep peaceably in their beds at night only because rough men stand ready to do violence on their behalf."

—George Orwell

"Lead me, follow me, or get
the hell out of my way."

— George S. Patton Jr.

"Courage is the most important of all the virtues because without courage, you can't practice any other virtue consistently."

— Maya Angelou

"Family is not an important
thing. It's everything."

—Michael J. Fox

"The day the soldiers stop bringing you their problems is the day you stopped leading them. They have either lost confidence that you can help them or concluded that you do not care. Either case is a failure of leadership."

— Colin Powell

"To handle yourself, use your head; to handle others, use your heart."

— Eleanor Roosevelt

"It is fatal to enter a war
without the will to win it."

— Douglas MacArthur

"The bond that links your true family is not one of blood, but of respect and joy in each other's life."

—Richard Bach

"Courage is found in unlikely places."

— J.R.R. Tolkien

"Leadership is about being a servant first."

—Allen West

"Without continual growth
and progress, such words as
improvement, achievement,
and success have no
meaning."

— Benjamin Franklin

"America's finest - our men and women in uniform, are a force for good throughout the world, and that is nothing to apologize for."

— Sarah Palin

"The experience I gained from serving in the United States Air Force was crucial when it came to me working in the civilian world. I felt light years ahead of my co-workers."

—Curt Thomas

"Most of the important things in the world have been accomplished by people who have kept on trying when there seemed to be no hope at all."

—Dale Carnegie

"Courage is not the absence of fear, but rather the judgement that something else is more important than fear."

— Ambrose Redmoon

"I can imagine no more rewarding a career. And any man who may be asked in this century what he did to make his life worthwhile, I think can respond with a good deal of pride and satisfaction: 'I served in the United States Navy."

— John F. Kennedy

"America without her Soldiers would be like God without His angels."

— Claudia Pemberton

"Coming together is a beginning; keeping together is progress; working together is success."

—Henry Ford

"If you're walking down the right path and you're willing to keep walking, eventually you'll make progress."

—Barack Obama

"Soldiers can sometimes make decisions that are smarter than the orders they've been given."

— Orson Scott Card

"Two of my best friends and I left to go into the military after graduating high school. One when into the Army, the other into the Navy, and I joined the Air Force. The next year we saw each other, we all had different stories!"

—Curt Thomas

www.CurtThomasSpeaks.com

"I stand here before you not as a prophet, but as a humble servant of you, the people."

—Nelson Mandela

"It takes a great deal of bravery to stand up to our enemies, but just as much to stand up to our friends."

— J.K. Rowling

"Nothing will work unless you do."

—Maya Angelou

"There are no constraints on the human mind, no walls around the human spirit, no barriers to our progress except those we ourselves erect."

—Ronald Reagan

"All our chief wants is someone who will inspire us to be what we know we could be."

—Ralph Waldo Emerson

"My family was willing to sacrifice their time with me just so I could go to drill one weekend a month. It wasn't easy but I am forever grateful for their sacrifices as well."

—Curt Thomas

"Success is not final, failure is not fatal: it is the courage to continue that counts."

— Winston S. Churchill

"Don't be afraid of your fears. They're not there to scare you. They're there to let you know that something is worth it."

— C. JoyBell C.

"Those who served, and those who continue to serve in the Army, Navy, Air Force, Marines, and Coast Guard took an oath to uphold and protect the Constitution against all enemies foreign and domestic, and we can never forget the importance of their commitment to our Nation."

—Robin Hayes

"Restlessness is discontent and discontent is the first necessity of progress. Show me a thoroughly satisfied man and I will show you a failure."

—Thomas A. Edison

"Family means no one gets
left behind or forgotten."

—David Ogden Stiers

"Confront the dark parts of yourself, and work to banish them with illumination and forgiveness. Your willingness to wrestle with your demons will cause your angels to sing."

— August Wilson

"People won't totally understand what it really means to be free in America until they serve in the military."

—Curt Thomas

"A ship is safe in harbor, but that's not what ships are for."

— William G.T. Shedd

"Nothing ever comes to one,
that is worth having, except as
a result of hard work."

— Booker T. Washington

"Without fear there cannot be courage."

— Christopher Paolini

"He who rejects change is the architect of decay. The only human institution which rejects progress is the cemetery."

—Harold Wilson

"Every time you tear a leaf off a calendar, you present a new place for new ideas and progress."

—Charles Kettering

"Only one man in a thousand
is a leader of men--the other
999 follow women."

—Groucho Marx

"Freedom lies in being bold."

— Robert Frost

"I learned that courage was not the absence of fear, but the triumph over it. The brave man is not he who does not feel afraid, but he who conquers that fear."

— Nelson Mandela

"One person with a belief is equal to ninety-nine who have only interests."

—John Stuart Mill

"You have to defend your honor. And your family."

—Suzanne Veg

"Patriotism is voluntary. It is a feeling of loyalty and allegiance that is the result of knowledge and belief. A patriot shows their patriotism through their actions, by their choice."

—Jesse Ventura

"Courage isn't having the strength to go on - it is going on when you don't have strength."

— Napoléon Bonaparte

"I can tell if someone served in the military. We all have that 'spirit' that is noticeable from across the room. You had to have served to know what I'm talking about."

—Curt Thomas

"No matter how long you train someone to be brave, you never know if they are or not until something real happens."

— Veronica Roth

"Courage is grace under pressure."

— Ernest Hemingway

"The secret of happiness is freedom, the secret of freedom is courage."

— Carrie Jones

"I never had a sister until I joined the military!"

—Curt Thomas

""A leader takes people where they want to go. A great leader takes people where they don't necessarily want to go, but ought to be."

—Rosalynn Carter

"Believe you can and you're halfway there."

— Theodore Roosevelt

"Courage is being scared to death, but saddling up anyway."

— John Wayne

"Keep in mind that many people have died for their beliefs; it's actually quite common. The real courage is in living and suffering for what you believe."

— Christopher Paolini

"Every time I see a military ember, especially a veteran, I try to make every effort to shake their hand and extend my appreciation for their service. They deserve more than that and we all know it."

—Curt Thomas

"Don't bother people for help without first trying to solve the problem yourself."

—Colin Powell

"A man with outward courage dares to die; a man with inner courage dares to live."

— Lao Tzu

"Man cannot discover new oceans unless he has the courage to lose sight of the shore."

— André Gide

"One's dignity may be assaulted, vandalized and cruelly mocked, but it can never be taken away unless it is surrendered."

— Michael J. Fox

"There is an unique brotherhood and sisterhood when a veteran meets another veteran. We feel like family even if it's our first time meeting one another."

—Curt Thomas

"To share your weakness is to make yourself vulnerable; to make yourself vulnerable is to show your strength."

— Criss Jami

"It is not the strength of the body that counts, but the strength of the spirit."

— J.R.R. Tolkien

"You cannot swim for new horizons until you have courage to lose sight of the shore."

— William Faulkner

"Hardships make or break
people."

— Margaret Mitchell

"We cannot be sure of having something to live for unless we are willing to die for it."

— Che Guevara

"Courage is not simply one of the virtues but the form of every virtue at the testing point, which means at the point of highest reality."

— C.S. Lewis

"We are shaped by our thoughts; we become what we think. When the mind is pure, joy follows like a shadow that never leaves."

—Buddha

"Never neglect details. When everyone's mind is dulled or distracted the leader must be doubly vigilant."

— Colin Powell

"There is no substitute for
hard work."

—Thomas A. Edison

"The love of family and the admiration of friends is much more important than wealth and privilege."

—Charles Kuralt

"My wingman assigned to me when I entered back into the Air Force Reserves was a female. She's my sister now. She's a leader, supporter, and loyal. That's more than I could say about most guys!"

—Curt Thomas

"Great achievement is usually born of great sacrifice, and is never the result of selfishness."

—Napoleon Hill

"A team will always appreciate a great individual if he's willing to sacrifice for the group."

—Kareem Abdul-Jabbar

"It is not sacrifice if you love
what you're doing."

—Mia Hamm

"I have long believed that sacrifice is the pinnacle of patriotism."

—Bob Riley

"Freedom is a right ultimately defended by the sacrifice of America's servicemen and women."

—Arnold Schwarzenegger

"Be ashamed to die until you
have won some victory for
humanity."

—Horace Mann

"Doing nothing for others is

the undoing of ourselves."

—Horace Mann

"The healthiest competition occurs when average people win by putting above average effort."

—Colin Powell

"My father told me once that
the most important thing
every man should know is
what he would die for."

— Tana French

"Anything that you cannot sacrifice pins you. Makes you predictable, makes you weak."

— Mark Lawrence

"They never fail who die in a great cause."

— George Gordon Byron

"If you're not ready to die for
it, put the word 'freedom' out
of your vocabulary."

—Malcolm X

"Find a place inside where there's joy, and the joy will burn out the pain."

—Joseph Campbell

"All the great things are simple, and many can be expressed in a single word: freedom, justice, honor, duty, mercy, hope."

—Winston Churchill

"We must all suffer one of two things: the pain of discipline or the pain of regret or disappointment."

—Jim Rohn

"When you have to cope with a lot of problems, you're either going to sink or you're going to swim."

—Tom Cruise

"A flower cannot blossom without sunshine, and man cannot live without love."

—Max Muller

"Leadership is the art of getting someone else to do something you want done because he wants to do it."

—Dwight D. Eisenhower

"Being entirely honest with oneself is a good exercise."

—Sigmund Freud

"Victory has a hundred fathers
and defeat is an orphan."

— John F. Kennedy

"The greatest way to live with honor in this world is to be what we pretend to be."

—Socrates

"Management is doing things right; leadership is doing the right things."

— Peter F. Drucker

"If you want to conquer fear, don't sit home and think about it. Go out and get busy."

—Dale Carnegie

"Example is not the main thing in influencing others. It is the only thing."

— Albert Schweitzer

"Leaders must be close enough to relate to others, but far enough ahead to motivate them."

— John C. Maxwell

"The mark of a great man is one who knows when to set aside the important things in order to accomplish the vital ones."

—Brandon Sanderson

"Leadership is not about titles, positions, or flow charts. It is about one life influencing another."

—John C. Maxwell

"You have to be burning with an idea, or a problem, or a wrong that you want to right. If you're not passionate enough from the start, you'll never stick it out."

— Steve Jobs

"Service which is rendered without joy helps neither the servant nor the served. But all other pleasures and possessions pale into nothingness before service which is rendered in a spirit of joy."

—Mahatma Gandhi

"I put forth the same energy while at reserve drill as I did working as a state trooper. Even on days when I left the highway to go straight to the base the night before drill. The way I saw it, if these other reservists can come here from their full-time jobs and give a 100%, so should I."
—Curt Thomas

"The best executive is the one who has sense enough to pick good men to do what he wants done, and self-restraint to keep from meddling with them while they do it."

—Theodore Roosevelt

"I don't see myself being special; I just see myself having more responsibilities than the next man. People look to me to do things for them, to have answers."

— Tupac Shakur

"If you would convince a man that he does wrong, do right. But do not care to convince him. Men will believe what they see. Let them see."

—Henry David Thoreau

"The healthiest competition occurs when average people win by putting above average effort."

—Colin Powell

"I cannot trust a man to control others who cannot control himself."

— Robert E. Lee

"Service which is rendered
without joy helps neither the
servant nor the served. But all
other pleasures and
possessions pale into
nothingness before service
which is rendered in a spirit of
joy."

—Mahatma Gandhi

"'Give as few orders as possible,' his father had told him once long ago. 'Once you've given orders on a subject, you must always give orders on that subject.'"

— Frank Herbert

"I have but one lamp by which
my feet are guided, and that is
the lamp of experience."

—Patrick Henry

"You can change your world
by changing your words...
Remember, death and life are
in the power of the tongue."

—Joel Osteen

"The art of leadership is saying no, not yes. It is very easy to say yes."

— Tony Blair

"People may hear your words,
but they feel your attitude."

— John C. Maxwell

"Don't tell people how to do things, tell them what to do and let them surprise you with their results."

—George Patton

"Only those who have learned the power of sincere and selfless contribution experience life's deepest joy: true fulfillment."

—Tony Robbins

"Take advantage of every opportunity to practice your communication skills so that when important occasions arise, you will have the gift, the style, the sharpness, the clarity, and the emotions to affect other people."

—Jim Rohn

"The price of success is hard work, dedication to the job at hand, and the determination that whether we win or lose, we have applied the best of ourselves to the task at hand."

—Vince Lombardi

"You can do what you have to do, and sometimes you can do it even better than you think you can."

—Jimmy Carter

"If you set goals and go after them with all the determination you can muster, your gifts will take you places that will amaze you."

—Les Brown

"Besides your immediate
family at home, you won't find
another family in the world
that this close. The members
you serve with are your
extended family."

—Curt Thomas

The COURAGE to SERVE

www.CurtThomasSpeaks.com

Thank you all for your service and sacrifice...

The COURAGE to SERVE

Like us on Facebook:

Keyword: Curt Thomas Motivational Speaker

Instagram:

Keyword: @CurtThomasSpeaks

Follow on Twitter:

Keyword: @CurtSpeaks

www.ingramcontent.com/pod-product-compliance
Lightning Source LLC
Chambersburg PA
CBHW070810050426
42452CB00011B/1982